SPAIN
the people

Noa Lior and Tara Steele

A Bobbie Kalman Book

The Lands, Peoples, and Cultures Series

Crabtree Publishing Company
www.crabtreebooks.com

W

The Lands, Peoples, and Cultures Series

Created by Bobbie Kalman

Coordinating editor
Ellen Rodger

Production coordinator
Rosie Gowsell

Project development, photo research, and design
First Folio Resource Group, Inc.
  Erinn Banting
  Tom Dart
  Söğüt Y. Güleç
  Claire Milne
  Debbie Smith

Editing
Carolyn Black

Separations and film
Embassy Graphics

Printer
Worzalla Publishing Company

Consultants
Bredan Ara; Mike Ara; José Félix Barrio, Adviser, Ministry of Education, Culture and Sport of Spain; Isaac Hernández

Photographs
J. Bardajil/MercuryPress.com: p. 31; Clement/Explorer/Photo Researchers: p. 13 (left); Stuart Cohen/The Image Works: p. 22 (top); Corbis/Magma Photo News Inc./Agence France Presse: p. 25 (top); Corbis/Magma Photo News Inc./Edifice: p. 3; Corbis/Magma Photo News Inc./Owen Franken: p. 22 (bottom); Corbis/Magma Photo News Inc./Gianni Dagli Orti: p. 6; Corbis/Magma Photo News Inc./Reuters NewMedia Inc.: p. 10 (left); Corbis/Magma Photo News Inc./Galen Rowell: p. 11 (bottom); Corbis/Magma Photo News Inc./Patrick Ward: title page; Corbis/Magma Photo News Inc./Julia Waterlow: p. 30 (right); Corbis/Magma Photo News Inc./Nik Wheeler: p. 12 (left), p. 19 (top); J. L. Cuesta/MercuryPress.com: p. 11 (top); Sonda Dawes/The Image Works: p. 26 (top); Chad Ehlers/International Stock: p. 13 (right); Esbin-Anderson/The Image Works: p. 16 (right); Macduff Everton/The Image Works: p. 27 (both); David Frazier/The Image Works: p. 28 (bottom); Beryl Goldberg: p. 20 (right), p. 21 (top), p. 26 (bottom), p. 28 (top); Ned Haines/Photo Researchers: cover; Blaine Harrington III: p. 25 (bottom); Isaac Hernández/MercuryPress.com: p. 16 (left), p. 23 (top), p. 30 (left); Hulton Archive by Getty Images: p. 7 (bottom), p. 10 (right); Emma Lee/Life File: p. 14 (bottom), p. 15 (top), p. 18 (top), p. 29; MercuryPress.com: p. 14 (top), p. 17 (both); North Wind Pictures: p. 7 (top), p. 8 (both), p. 9 (both); David Peevers: p. 15 (bottom), p. 24; J. A. Sanchez/MercuryPress.com: p. 4 (top); Paul Stepan/Photo Researchers: p. 5 (bottom); Paul Thompson/International Stock: p. 18 (bottom); Flora Torrance/Life File: p. 12 (right); Ulrike Welsch: p. 4 (bottom), p. 5 (top), p. 19 (bottom), p. 20 (left), p. 21 (bottom), p. 23 (bottom)

Illustrations
Dianne Eastman: icon
David Wysotski, Allure Illustrations: back cover

Cover: A woman gathers small purple flowers, called crocuses, near Albacete, in eastern Spain. The stigmas, or centers, of crocuses are used to make an expensive spice called saffron.

Title page: Horse-drawn carts carry people through the Plaza de España in Seville, in southern Spain. People visit the *plaza* to see its beautiful buildings and fountains.

Icon: Homes made of mud bricks dried in the sun, which are found in many of Spain's towns and villages, appear at the head of each section.

Back cover: The Hierro giant lizard lives in nature reserves such as the Coto Doñana.

Published by
Crabtree Publishing Company

PMB 16A,	612 Welland Avenue	73 Lime Walk
350 Fifth Avenue	St. Catharines	Headington
Suite 3308	Ontario, Canada	Oxford OX3 7AD
New York	L2M 5V6	United Kingdom
N.Y. 10118		

Cataloging in Publication Data
Lior, Noa, 1693-
    Spain. The people / Noa Lior and Tara Steele.
    p. cm. -- (The lands, peoples, and cultures series)
    Includes index.
    Summary: Examines the history of Spain and its peoples, religions, languages, and ways of life
    ISBN 0-7787-9365-6 (RLB) -- ISBN 0-7787-9733-3 (pbk.)
    1. Spain--Social life and customs--Juvenile literature. [1. Spain.]
I. Title. II. Series.
    HN583.5.L55 2002
    j946   2001903121-1
                                                    LC

Contents

Different traditions

When people think of Spain, they sometimes imagine bullfighters, black-haired **flamenco** dancers, fishers, and olive farmers. While these traditional images are still a part of Spanish life, the people who live in Spain today are just as likely to be working in a modern office, talking on a cell phone, or enjoying a nice meal with friends in an outdoor café.

Regional lifestyles

Each region in Spain is home to a distinct group of people that speaks its own language and practices centuries-old **customs**. Many Spaniards feel stronger ties to the region where they live than to the country as a whole. For example, people from the Basque territory, in the north of Spain, or Catalonia, in the northeast, often describe themselves as Basques or Catalans first, and Spaniards second.

(right) Riding a donkey is one way to get to an outdoor market in southern Spain.

(top) Bullfighting is a very popular sport in Spain. During a bullfight, picadores on horseback weaken huge bulls by stabbing lances into their backs.

Two girls jot down notes about Barcelona's cathedral, La Seu, during a class trip.

*The Plaza del Castillo is the main **plaza**, or square, in Pamplona, in northern Spain. People go to the **plaza** to shop, take a stroll, or meet with friends at one of the many cafés.*

Layers of history

In 1868, a farmer discovered paintings in a cave in the Cantabrian Mountains, in northern Spain. He told a man from nearby Santander about them because he knew the man was interested in history. Ten years later, the man from Santander brought his nine-year-old daughter to investigate the caves. His daughter became bored and started swinging her lantern. When the light bounced off the ceiling, she cried, "Look, Papá, painted oxen!"

The pictures that the young girl found in the Altamira caves date from 15,000 to 8500 B.C. They show bison, wild boars, and other animals that people hunted at that time. They were painted by the first people to live in Spain and are considered some of the finest examples of cave art anywhere in the world.

Settling in

The next known people to live in Spain were the Iberians. They came from northern Africa, crossing the Mediterranean Sea into Spain around 3000 B.C. They built small towns and villages, where they farmed the land and worked as skilled metalworkers, potters, and sculptors. About 2,000 years later, the Celts came to Spain from Europe, finding their way across the rugged Pyrenees mountains in the north. After settling in Galicia, in northwest Spain, they began to raise **livestock** and farm the land.

Only 30 people are allowed to visit the Altamira caves each day because the warmth that comes from people's body temperature can damage the pictures, such as this painting of a bison.

Phoenicians and Greeks

Phoenicians from the eastern Mediterranean came to Spain around 1000 B.C. and settled along the east coast. They came in search of valuable minerals such as gold, silver, tin, and copper. A few centuries later, Greeks arrived and settled in the northeast. Both the Phoenician and Greek settlers shipped Spanish food, fish, salt, minerals, and pottery back to people in their **homelands**. They also introduced many foods from their homelands to Spain, such as grapes and olives, which are still grown in Spain today.

Carthaginians and Romans

Armies from Carthage, in northern Africa, began arriving in Spain after 400 B.C. in search of territory to **occupy**. Then, in 206 B.C., Romans came to Spain to fight the Carthaginians for control of the area. They won the battle and imposed common laws and a single language, Latin, on most of the land. During the next 600 years, waves of Romans came to live in Spain, where they built cities, temples, outdoor theaters, roads, and **aqueducts**. Some of the people from Rome were Christians, while others were Jews. Christians follow the teachings of Jesus Christ, whom they believe is the son of God. Jewish people follow the teachings of God, which are written in their holy book, the *Torah*.

Visigoths

By 400 A.D., tribes from northern Europe began attacking Spain. One of these tribes, the Visigoths, defeated the Romans in Spain in 409 and took control of the northern part of the country. The Visigoth kings adopted Christianity from the Romans, and forced Jewish citizens to convert to Christianity. The next 300 years were a dark period in Spain's history, marked by battles in different regions and a lack of law and order. Cities began to fall apart. The country was weak and vulnerable to **invasion**.

(above) In this drawing from the 1300s, Phoenician traders cross the Mediterranean Sea on a boat that is paddled with very long oars.

In this drawing, an army of Visigoths attack a village near Toledo, in central Spain.

(above) *The ancient mosque in Córdoba, shown in this painting, was built by the Moors during the 700s. Today, it is a Roman Catholic cathedral, but remains one of the most beautiful examples of Moorish architecture in Spain.*

Moors and Islam

The Moors, from northern Africa, landed at Gibraltar, in the south of Spain, in 711. It took them less than seven years to conquer all of Spain, except for a few Christian kingdoms in the north. The Moors ruled Spain for the next 800 years. They settled mainly in the southern part of the country, in a region now known as Andalusia.

The Moors had an enormous influence on life in Spain. Farmland flourished when the Moors introduced sophisticated methods of **irrigation**. The Moors built beautiful palaces, public baths, schools, and gardens. They introduced the religion of Islam, practiced by Muslims, to Spain. Muslims believe in one god, *Allah*, and his **prophet**, Muhammad. Many Spanish people became Muslims during the Moors' rule, although the Moors allowed Christians and Jews to follow their own religious beliefs. The Moors were also very knowledgeable about math and science. Under the Moors, Spain became a center of learning and **culture**.

Reconquest

Eventually, the Christian kingdoms in the north began a long fight to win the country back from the Moors. This period, from 718 to 1491, is known as the Reconquest. The two most powerful kingdoms in northern Spain were Castile and Aragon. When Queen Isabella of Castile and King Ferdinand of Aragon married in 1469, they united their forces. Isabella and Ferdinand finally drove the Moors out of the country when they captured the kingdom of Granada, the Moors' last stronghold, in 1492.

In this painting from the late 1400s, King Ferdinand and Queen Isabella, accompanied by a small army, arrive at the palace of the Moors in Granada, after the Moors surrendered the kingdom.

The Spanish Inquisition

Ferdinand and Isabella practiced a **denomination** of Christianity called Roman Catholicism. They insisted that everyone in Spain also practice Catholicism. **Mosques** and **synagogues** were destroyed and rebuilt as churches. Jews and Muslims were given a choice: convert to Catholicism or leave the country. Those who chose to convert were still **persecuted**. For example, Muslim converts were forced to live in certain rural areas. In 1478, Ferdinand and Isabella set up the Inquisition, a court to investigate whether people were practicing Roman Catholicism. People who

had not converted or whose beliefs were questioned were sent out of the country, punished severely, or **executed**. Five thousand people were executed in the first 50 years of the Inquisition, which finally ended in 1834.

A prisoner stands before King Ferdinand and a jury of priests at a trial during the Spanish Inquisition, in this drawing from the 1800s.

Explorers and conquerors

In 1492, Queen Isabella paid for an Italian explorer, Christopher Columbus, to search for a new route to India by water. She wanted easier access to India's spices and other riches. When Columbus's ship landed on one of the islands of the Bahamas, instead of India, he became the first European explorer to see this part of America. After Columbus's return, Queen Isabella gave money to other Spanish explorers, so they could bring the riches of the Americas back to Spain. These Spanish adventurers, or *conquistadores*, gradually conquered Mexico, Central America, parts of the United States, and parts of South America. From these conquered **territories**, they shipped gold, jewels, and precious metals, as well as cocoa, corn, and potatoes, to Spain, making it one of the wealthiest nations in the world.

This etching shows a battle between the Spanish Armada and the British navy, which took place in 1588. Over 30,000 Spanish fighters died during this battle.

The Spanish Armada

In 1588, the king of Spain sent a fleet of 133 ships, called the Armada, to invade England. Almost half these ships sank in stormy weather or while fighting the British navy. This was a major defeat for Spain, and it marked the beginning of a slow decline in Spain's power. One by one, Spain's overseas territories regained their independence.

The Spanish Civil War

For hundreds of years, Spain was a monarchy, ruled by kings and queens. In 1931, Spain became a republic in which the citizens elected their government. People who supported this new government were called Republicans. In 1936, General Francisco Franco led the Spanish army in an uprising against the new government because he wanted the country to be run in an older, traditional way. Franco and the people fighting with him were called Nationalists.

Civil war shook the country for more than three years, killing over half-a-million people. Almost as many people fled from Spain to other countries. Eventually, the Nationalists won the war, and Franco made himself leader of the nation.

General Franco's rule

Franco was a dictator, a leader who ruled with absolute authority and force. He **abolished** the **parliament**, leaving only one political party —his own. Franco was also a fascist. Fascists believe that a country can only be strong if the government restricts peoples' rights and freedoms. One of the ways Franco did this was by allowing people in Spain to speak only Castilian, the language spoken in central Spain. People living in different parts of the country were not allowed to speak their own languages or practice their own customs.

Following World War II, General Franco passed a series of laws to protect his power. The Law of Succession, passed in 1947, declared that General Franco would rule until his death and decide who would be Spain's next leader.

King Juan Carlos

General Franco chose Juan Carlos to rule after him, as king. Juan Carlos's grandfather, Alfonso XIII, had been king of Spain from 1886 to 1931. Franco thought that Juan Carlos would continue his fascist policies. Instead, after Franco died in 1975, Juan Carlos appointed a new prime minister and helped establish a democracy in Spain. Elections were held in 1977, and Spaniards chose who they wanted to govern them. Today, Spain continues to have an elected prime minister and strong parliament, as well as a monarch.

King Juan Carlos (right) speaks to prime minister Jose Maria Anzar before a meeting in 1999 with members of the Spanish parliament on the island of Majorca, off the eastern coast of Spain.

Almost 40 million people live in Spain. For hundreds of years, the largest group has been the Castilian people. They live mainly in two regions in central Spain called Castilla-León and Castilla-La Mancha. Most Castilians live in major cities such as Madrid or Toledo, but some still live in small farming communities. Castilians have a strong influence on Spain's politics because of their great numbers. Their language, Castilian, is the official language of Spain.

Basques

The Basque people live in the north of Spain and the south of France. Many people believe that the Basques are descended from the very first people to live on the Iberian Peninsula, where Spain is located. The Basques have their own language, Euskera, and their own dances, songs, and poetry. The traditional games they play, such as *harikela*, where men compete by lifting massive stones, reflect their close ties to the land. In the past, Basques were often farmers and sailors, but today many of them work in mines and factories.

Hundreds of years ago, when Spain and France were made up of small, separate kingdoms or states, the Basques lived together in one kingdom called Navarra. When Spain and France became countries, Navarra was split between them. Since then, the Basques have fought for, and won, some power to rule themselves. Today, groups of Basques continue to struggle for independence. One group wants the Basque lands in Spain and France to become a separate nation. This group is called the ETA, which stands for *Euskadi Ta Askatasuna* and means "Basque Homeland and Freedom." The ETA regularly uses violence to draw attention to its views. Its **terrorist** acts have killed hundreds of people and caused many Basques to stop supporting the ETA's beliefs.

(above) Castilian shoppers crowd a main street in Madrid.

Basque farmers watch over their flock of sheep near Ceanuri, a village in the Pyrenees.

11

Galicians

Galicians are descended from the Celts, who came to Spain from Europe almost 3,000 years ago. Galicians live near the sea in the northwest part of the country, in a region called Galicia. They are great fishers and sailors. They speak their own language, Gallego, in addition to Castilian. Galicians love writing poetry in Gallego and playing music on Celtic instruments called *gaitas*, which resemble bagpipes. The music and dances of Galicia are similar to those of Scotland and Ireland because the people of these three places all have Celtic **ancestors**.

A Catalan woman, who has just bought fresh peppers, broccoli, onions, and carrots, gets change from a vendor at an outdoor market in Barcelona.

Catalans

Catalans live in Catalonia, in the northeast part of Spain. Farmers in this region grow wheat, corn, oranges, and grapes, and raise pigs and goats. On the coast, people fish, manufacture textiles, make wine, or work in the region's major book publishing industry. Catalonia's unique history and culture was recognized in 1977 when it was granted limited autonomy, or the right to govern itself.

Although Phoenicians and Greeks settled first in this area, the greatest influence on Catalan culture came from the French, who conquered and ruled over the territory at different times during the 1600s and 1800s. The influence of the French can be seen in the Catalan language, which is more closely related to a southern French **dialect** than to Spanish.

People of Andalusia

The people of Andalusia, in the south, are the descendants of the Moors who came to Spain from Africa. Andalusian culture has had a strong influence on life in the rest of the country. Flamenco guitar music and flamenco dancing began in Andalusia, but they are now popular throughout Spain and the world. Bullfighting, another traditional Spanish pastime, also comes from Andalusia.

*A Galician man, dressed in traditional costume, prepares to play a **gaita** at the Festival of St. James in Santiago de Compostela, in the northwest. Each year, on July 25, the city welcomes thousands of visitors for the festival.*

Other peoples

When Franco ruled Spain, many Spaniards **immigrated** to other countries in search of a better life. Once Franco died, people from other countries started immigrating to Spain. Now, about one million Latin Americans, Africans, Asians, Eastern Europeans, and Middle-Eastern Europeans live in Spain. It is quite common to see people from all over the world living in big cities such as Madrid.

Gitanos

Gitanos, or Gypsies, have lived in Spain for over 500 years. People believe they came to Spain from northwestern India during the 1400s to escape fighting between invading peoples. In the past, *Gitanos* traveled in **caravans** and were a nomadic people, meaning they traveled from place to place. Most lived in the south of Spain, where the warm weather made an outdoor way of life easier. Now, many live in cities such as Madrid and Barcelona. *Gitanos* often face **discrimination**, and experience high levels of unemployment and poverty. The Spanish government has set up programs to help them tackle these challenges. As well, many *Gitanos* have formed political organizations to bring about change, and some have been elected to parliament.

*A **Gitano** girl, wearing brightly colored earrings, waits for her friends at El Rastro, an outdoor market in Madrid, the capital of Spain.*

🏠 Village life 🏠

Small villages dot Spain's countryside. Many were built on top of hills during times of conflict, so villagers could see danger coming from far away. Unfortunately, these hilltop villages are also far from big cities. People who live there must sometimes travel a long way to find services they need, such as hospitals.

The heart of the village

Village houses sit close together with very small gardens behind them. Some houses are made of mud brick, or adobe. In the middle of many Spanish villages is a main square, which is called the *plaza mayor*. The *plaza mayor* is the center of public life in the village, and it is where the town hall and the church are usually located. Markets and special events or celebrations, such as *fiestas*, take place in this square. People also meet there to talk or take a walk, called a *paseo*.

(above) Shops and restaurants surround Las Ramblas, the main square of Figueras, a town on the eastern coast.

(top) Puente Viesgo, a village in the north, sits amid the valleys of the Cantabrian Mountains.

Getting around

Most Spanish villages were built before people had cars. Some of the streets are too narrow for vehicles, but just the right size for people on foot or for donkeys, which are sometimes used to transport people or goods. Roads wide enough for cars and trucks wind around the newer houses, stores, and other businesses that spring up on the edges of villages, where land is available.

Handpainted dishes, bowls, and vases cover a table at a market in Empuribrava, a town in the east.

Three friends sit on a park bench in Zamora, in central Spain, to chat, watch passersby, and enjoy the sunny weather.

Life in the village

Life in Spain's villages has changed a great deal over the years. Farmers used to spend their days in the fields surrounding the village, while other villagers worked closer to home at tasks such as repairing buildings, digging irrigation ditches, or making crafts. After lunch, when it was too hot to work outside, villagers would stay indoors and take a nap, or *siesta*, before returning to work.

Today, some villagers continue to farm, although most are older and retired. They spend their days socializing in the *plaza mayor*, gardening, and shopping at small shops and outdoor markets where farmers sell fruit and vegetables. Villagers continue to make pottery and weave, producing crafts that they sell to tourists. The reason today's villages have fewer farmers and young people is that many children decide they do not want to farm as their parents did. Instead, they sell the family land to other farmers or to people who develop it for the tourism industry. Then, they move to the cities to attend university and find work. Some families live in the city during the school year and only return to their village for the holidays. Other families live in the city, while the father travels back and forth to the village to run a farm.

In many ways, Spain's large cities look the same as large cities around the world. Skyscrapers tower over elegant hotels, traffic clogs streets, and people hurry by, listening to their portable CD players. At the same time, life in Spanish cities is an interesting mix of the old and the new. Tall buildings sit beside small open markets, while remains of ancient Roman walls appear to stand guard over busy industrial **ports**.

Old buildings and modern skyscrapers crowd the skyline in Barcelona, the second-largest city in Spain.

The shape of the city

Many modern Spanish cities were founded long ago. Architectural ruins from the time of the Moors and Romans can still be seen in the "old quarter," or *casco viego*, of many cities. Here, narrow streets and small buildings crowd together. Delicious smells from small restaurants and bars compete with tempting displays of fresh fruit, vegetables, and other foods in many of the cities' best markets. In the newer areas built around the *casco viego*, roads are wider, buildings are taller, and there are more businesses.

A lot of people

With so many people moving to cities, housing has become a problem. Some single-family houses exist in places such as Barcelona or Madrid, but only the very wealthy can afford them. Most people live in apartments built above restaurants and stores in the center of cities, or in high-rise condominiums in the **suburbs**.

Apartment buildings, restaurants, and small shops that sell food, clothing, and jewelry fill this **casco viego** *of Toledo.*

Cars jam a highway on the outskirts of Madrid. Some mornings, rush-hour traffic is so bad that it can take hours for people to get in and out of the city.

Traffic

Spanish cities suffer from traffic jams, limited parking space, and the pollution that comes from too many cars, but governments are finding solutions to these problems. Cities such as Barcelona and Madrid have well-planned subway systems and bus routes. During the day, certain streets in Madrid are open only to buses, taxis, or trucks making deliveries, but not to cars. In Barcelona, cars are not allowed to park on some of the busier main streets during the day. In some cities, no matter what time of day, cars are restricted from driving on the narrow streets of the old quarter. These streets are for pedestrians only.

The *paseo*

While villagers tend to meet in the *plaza mayor*, people who live in cities often get together at the *paseo*. *Paseo* refers to both a walkway and going for a walk. Almost every city has a *paseo*, a wide, paved strip in the middle of a main downtown road with benches, trees, sidewalk cafés, and stalls selling books, newspapers, or fruit.

*After work or after dinner, the **paseo** is crowded with friends getting together to talk, shop, or relax.*

Going out

Spanish cities are exciting places, especially for people who enjoy staying up late at night. People go to concerts and plays, or watch the movies of famous Spanish filmmakers such as Pedro Almodóvar. They attend lectures and book readings. They meet friends in bars and restaurants, or go to music and dance clubs, where the real nightlife often does not pick up until after two o'clock in the morning!

School

Many children who are younger than six years old attend preschool or daycare before attending a **Centro de Educación General Básica.**

Buildings marked *Centro de Educación General Básica* appear in cities, towns, and large villages. These buildings are schools for students between the ages of six and sixteen. Most Spanish students go to these schools, which the government pays for and runs, but one-third go to private schools that their families pay for. The Catholic Church runs many of the private schools.

The school day

The school day begins at nine o'clock and lasts until five. Students take classes in mathematics, geography, history, science, Spanish, English, and another foreign language, such as French, German, or Italian. They also take art, music, and physical education. Students have a two-hour break, between one and three o'clock, for lunch and recess. Some of them go home to eat with their families, but most eat at school. By June, the hot afternoon weather makes it difficult for students to concentrate, so many schools hold classes only in the morning. In the summer, schools close for two-and-a-half to three months. Students also have vacations at Christmas, Easter, and for several other *fiestas*.

Taking a break

For fun, students play games, such as soccer or basketball, during breaks between classes and before and after school. In the early evening, after eating a snack, some children take lessons in English, soccer, or swimming, while others take courses in painting, ballet, chess, or tennis. Rally car and motocross racing are popular with students over the age of sixteen.

Choices

In Spain, children must stay in school until the age of sixteen. After this, they can continue with school, look for work, or enter a job-training program. Those who continue with school take the *bachillerato* course, which is two years long. At the end of the program, students write a set of exams. If they pass, they earn the title *bachiller*. Many of these graduates apply for university, for which they must write a difficult entrance exam that covers all subjects. Students who choose a job-training program instead of the *bachillerato* spend two to five years working and going to school part-time.

Students solve math problems during class in Barcelona.

School trips

Students look forward to the special trips that take place during the school year. In February, busloads of students and teachers from around the country crowd ski resorts for a few days of skiing called White Week. Other Spaniards stay away from the slopes at this time of year because they are so crowded! Students in their last year before the *bachillerato*, the last year of the *bachillerato*, and often in the third year of university also look forward to a study trip, or *viaje de estudios*. Study trips allow students to explore different parts of their country or neighboring countries such as France, Italy, or Portugal. Some trips are organized around a theme, such as castles or museums.

School trips are expensive, and students must raise money to pay for them. Often, a school buys hundreds of lottery tickets, and the students resell them at a slightly higher price. Another way to raise money is called *la carrera del duro*, or the nickel race. Students arrange four coins on the sidewalk in a large square. Then, they ask passersby for more coins to fill in the square. The bigger the square, the more money for the trip!

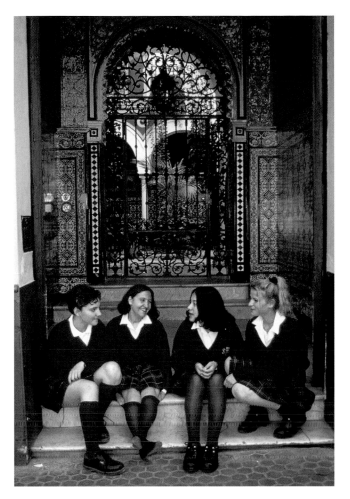

A group of girls from a private school tries to think of ways to raise money for their **viaje de estudios.**

Many students in Spain go to university after they complete the **bachillerato.** *These architecture students at the University of Barcelona sketch university buildings.*

Spaniards enjoy playing outdoor sports such as golf, baseball, basketball, tennis, and the most popular sport in Spain, soccer. In August, the cities are almost empty because so many people head for the mountains or the beaches, where they swim, sail, water ski, and windsurf. During the year, Spaniards enjoy several long weekends, when they take a break from their usual routine. A three-day weekend is called a bridge. A four-day weekend is called an aqueduct because it is longer!

Fútbol

Soccer is called *fútbol* in Spain. In every town, village, and city, both children and adults love practicing the game. When they are not playing in local leagues, they watch Spain's professional soccer teams compete against one another. Tens of thousands of people watch live soccer games at huge stadiums, and even more watch games on television. When Spain's national team plays in European or World Cup competitions, fans scream out encouragement and honk their car horns if their team wins. They think of the star players as superheroes!

Pelota vasca

Some people say that *pelota vasca*, which means "Basque ball," is the fastest game in the world. This form of handball was developed by the Basques. People first played it outside, on the walls of houses and sometimes against walls in the *plaza mayor*. Now, they commonly play on walled concrete courts called *frontones*.

The version of **pelota vasca** *played with a basket-type racket is called* **cesta punta**. *Today, people play* **cesta punta** *not only throughout Spain, but in countries such as Cuba, Mexico, the Philippines, and the United States, where it is known as* **jai alai**. *In the Basque language, Euskera,* **jai alai** *means "merry festival."*

(above) **Fútbol** *players try to keep the ball away from their opponents at a game in Ávila, in central Spain.*

Runners pass their baton to a teammate at a relay race on a high school track in Madrid.

How to play *pelota vasca*

Pelota vasca is played with a ball called a *pelota*, which is smaller and harder than a baseball. Two or four players hurl the *pelota* against the wall of the court. Each player tries to throw the ball against the wall in such a way that the other players cannot catch it. They throw and catch the ball with their bare hands, a hard paddle, or a racket called a *cesta*. The *cesta*, which is about 24 inches (60 centimeters) long, looks like a curved wicker basket and is strapped to the player's wrist. The curve of the *cesta* whips the ball at an incredible speed — up to 150 miles (240 kilometers) per hour!

Mountain sports

Spain's mountains are a favorite place for sports, no matter what time of year. In the summer, both Spaniards and tourists hike and mountain climb, while in the winter, they ski and snowboard. These activities are especially popular in the cold Pyrenees, as well as in the Sierra Nevada mountains in the south.

During their hike through the Sierra Nevada mountains in southern Spain, these people will see rugged mountain peaks, green valleys, and lush forests.

The bullfight

Spain is famous for its bullfights, a sport which dates back to the 1600s. Tens of thousands of people gather in bullfighting rings to watch brave *matadors* fight bulls. The bulls, which weigh about 1,100 pounds (500 kilograms) each, are bred and raised in Andalusia especially for bullfighting.

The art of the bullfight

Many Spanish people consider the bullfight an art form. A *matador* must have courage and skill to face the bull in the ring, but must also perform the correct moves with grace and flair. Part of this flair comes from the clothing. A *matador* wears a special costume called a *traje de luces*, or "suit of lights." This colorful outfit, which can cost as much as $10,000, consists of tights, tight pants, a wool hat, and a short jacket made of silk and embroidered with gold and silver sequins that glimmer in the sun. These jackets are incredibly heavy! A *matador* can lose up to three pounds (one kilogram) during a bullfight just from sweating!

The *corrida*

The bullfight, or *corrida*, has three parts. During the first part, called *tercio de Varas*, the *matador* parades around the bullfighting ring with a team of assistants. The bull enters the ring through the "gate of fear." *Picadores*, men riding horses, jab the bull in the neck with **lances** to weaken the animal. To test the bull's strength, the *matador* waves a large, red cape and watches how quickly the animal charges toward it.

The second part of the bullfight is called the *tercio de banderillas*. At this stage, men stick pointed darts decorated with ribbons into the bull's shoulders. These darts damage the bull's neck muscles, so it is difficult for the bull to raise its head suddenly and spear the *matador* with its horns.

(top) Before a bullfight in Seville, people dressed in traditional costumes ride through the ring in brightly colored wagons pulled by horses.

The *tercio de muleta*

The last stage of the bullfight is the *tercio de muleta*. Here, the *matador* dramatically teases the bull with his red cape, or *muleta*, trying to get the bull to come as close to his body as possible. The "moment of truth" comes when the *matador* thrusts his sword between the animal's shoulder blades, stabbing him through the heart. If the *matador* has performed well, and kills the bull cleanly and quickly, the crowd cheers and waves white handkerchiefs.

Banning bullfighting

Although bullfighting is still popular in Spain, especially among older people, many people in the country and in other parts of the world think killing an animal for sport is cruel. They believe that the bull suffers a slow, painful death, only for the viewers' entertainment. Animal protection groups around the world are trying to convince governments to ban bullfighting in Spain and other countries where it occurs, such as Mexico, Portugal, and Peru.

*Although most **matadors** are men, there have been a few female **matadors**, such as Christina Sanchez.*

*A **matador** teases a bull with his bright red cape. Many people think that the bull charges the cape because it is red. In fact, bulls are colorblind and will attack anything that moves.*

A taste of Spain

Spain's food is made with an interesting assortment of ingredients. Some ingredients are originally from Spain, while others were brought to the country by the different peoples who conquered it. Moors, for example, brought oranges, lemons, sugar, and rice from their African homeland. Spanish explorers brought chocolate, potatoes, peppers, and tomatoes back with them from conquered territories overseas.

Friends enjoy **churros,** *hot chocolate, and coffee at a café in Madrid.*

Time to eat

The hot weather in Spain forces many people to stay inside and rest for part of the day. This means that they stay up later at night. Over the course of their long day, Spaniards typically eat five times, instead of three. A hearty lunch is often the main meal.

Morning

Desayuno, or breakfast, is a simple meal of a fresh crusty loaf of bread, rolls called *bollos* or cookies called *galletas*, and a glass of milk, hot chocolate, or coffee. *Churros*, a kind of Spanish doughnut, are a popular breakfast treat. To make *churros*, strips of dough shaped like horseshoes or spirals are lightly fried and sprinkled with sugar.

Spaniards eat a snack around eleven o'clock in the morning called *almuerzo*. *Almuerzo* can be anything from a small dish of olives to a large plate of ham and eggs.

(top) A woman spoons out olives at a grocery store in Bilbao, in northern Spain. Olives are one of Spain's main crops.

Mortadela, tortillas española, *and fresh bread are all part of this family's meal at a restaurant in Pampaneira, in southern Spain.*

Midday

It is hottest in the middle of the day, so Spaniards come inside between one and three o'clock to eat and socialize. *La comida*, or lunch, usually has three courses, including a green salad, a chicken or meat dish, and fresh fruit for dessert. A popular lunch item is a *tortilla española*, which is a Spanish omelet made with eggs, potatoes, and onions. It is different from a Mexican *tortilla*, which is more like a flat pancake.

A mouthful

After work or school, Spaniards eat a light meal called *la merienda*. Children often eat a special sandwich called a *bocadillo*, which means "mouthful." A *bocadillo* is made with crusty bread filled with cheese, an omelet, or a cold meat which contains sliced olives called *mortadela*. Adults eat *la merienda* while chatting with friends at *tapas* bars or cafés. The little snacks called *tapas*, or "lids," were originally served on small saucers that sat on top of a drink.

Some favorite **tapas** *are olives, artichokes, Manchego cheese, shrimp in garlic sauce, and* **jamón serrano**, *which are pigs' legs. Flavorful pieces of fried squid or octopus are also available. Eating* **tapas** *is a Spanish tradition that people now enjoy in many parts of the world.*

Grocery stores and markets throughout Spain sell meats such as **mortadela** *and* **chorizo,** *a spicy pork sausage.*

Evening

Often, Spaniards do not eat dinner, or *la cena*, until nine or ten at night. *La cena* is not as large as lunch. It can be as simple as an omelet and a glass of milk.

In large cities, where many people cannot come home for lunch, dinner is the family's main meal. Stews with tomatoes, onions, beans, potatoes, carrots, sweet peppers, and garlic, along with meat or fish, are popular meals. All these ingredients cook together in a large pot, but they are often served separately. The liquid from the stew is served first, as a soup. Then, the vegetables are eaten. Finally, the meat or fish is dished out. This way, a single pot of stew provides a three-course meal.

Regional specialties

Each region in Spain has its own special dishes, which are made from local ingredients. Many dishes are relatively simple to prepare and are often cooked in one pot, like stew. In Galicia, where fishing is the main industry, people eat a lot of shellfish, including spider crabs, oysters, and scallops. *Fabada*, a stew made from beans and sausage, originated in Asturias, in the north of Spain. In central Spain, people eat wild game, such as partridge or pheasant, and lamb is regularly on the menu. Andalusia is the home of *gazpacho*, a cold soup made from mashed tomatoes and other vegetables, as well as olive oil. People in Castile make a hot soup with garlic and chunks of bread called *sopa de ajo castellana*. People in both Castile and Madrid enjoy a chickpea stew called *cocido*, which also includes vegetables such as potatoes, carrots, and onions, as well as meat such as *chorizo*.

Sardines, from the waters off the Mediterranean coast, are grilled over an open flame and eaten, or preserved in salt water or oil and canned.

Paella

Paella is a rice dish from the city of Valencia, on the east coast. Its yellow color comes from saffron, a spice made from the dried **stigmas** of the crocus flower. The other ingredients in *paella* vary from region to region, depending on what is available, but they sometimes include olives, red peppers, seafood, chicken, or pork. The iron pan in which *paella* is made is called a *paellera*. It is large, round, and shallow with a small handle on either side.

Roscón de reyes

Normally, desserts in Spain are quite simple. A meal often ends with fresh fruit, cookies, or sugar-coated almonds. There are, however, special desserts for special occasions, including *almendras garrapiñadas*, roasted almonds covered in caramel; *tortas*, a type of cake; and *rosquillas*, a type of doughnut. *Roscón de reyes*, or "crown of kings," is a round cake decorated with cream and candied fruit, which is fruit covered in sugar. People eat this cake at a religious holiday called Epiphany, twelve days after Christmas. Epiphany celebrates the three kings who brought gifts to the baby Jesus soon after he was born. Inside the cake is a lucky charm. Whoever gets the piece of cake with the charm will have good luck.

*At certain **fiestas**, people cook **paellas** in enormous **paelleras** over open fires. Three or four people are needed to stir these **paellas**!*

Arroz con leche

People all over Spain use rice in their cooking, even in desserts. *Arroz con leche*, or rice pudding, is a tasty dessert that is often served with fresh fruit or sprinkled with cinnamon. It is easy to make with an adult's help.

You will need:
6 cups (1.5 L) milk
1 cinnamon stick
2 or 3 strips lemon zest (fine peel)
pinch of salt
1/2 cup (125 ml) short-grain white rice
1/3 cup (75 ml) sugar
large saucepan
wooden spoon

What to do:
1. Pour the milk into a saucepan. Add the cinnamon stick, lemon zest, and salt. Heat to a boil. Stir in the rice.

2. Reduce heat to a simmer. Cook for 15 minutes, stirring constantly

3. Add the sugar.

4. Stirring occasionally, cook for 1 hour, or until the milk is absorbed and the pudding is very creamy and falls easily from the spoon. Add extra milk if the mixture is too thick.

5. Take out the cinnamon stick and lemon zest. Serve either warm, at room temperature, or slightly chilled.

This recipe makes enough *arroz con leche* to serve six people.

Antonia's alarm rings at 7:30 on Saturday morning. She has already been awake for an hour, staring out the window of her family's apartment in Barcelona. Antonia is excited because her aunt, uncle, and cousins, Gabriel and Marta, are coming from Falset, about an hour-and-a-half away. For a treat, Mamá is taking the family to a *fútbol* game. Barcelona's team, F. C. Barcelona or Barça for short, is playing against the team from Madrid, Real Madrid.

Antonia goes into the kitchen and finds her brother, Felipe, already there. She sneaks up behind him and shouts "*¡Hola!*" "*Buenos días,*" he greets her. "I heard you coming. Mamá bought us some *churros* before she left for work. I've been keeping them warm," he adds. Mamá works at a fancy hotel downtown. She is usually gone before Antonia and Felipe wake up.

A few hours later, Gabriel and Marta arrive with their parents. "*¡Hola* everyone!*" the cousins shout. Antonia's father thanks her aunt for the big pot of *gazpacho* she brought for lunch. "This is your first game at Camp Nou, isn't it, Antonia?" Gabriel asks. It's true, Antonia has never been to the giant stadium before. She can't imagine what it will be like to sit with 100,000 fans.

Like many families in Barcelona, Antonia, Felipe, and their parents live in an apartment building in the heart the city.

The family finishes eating around two o'clock, just as Mamá arrives home. She had a hard morning at work and goes to her room for a short *siesta* after she eats. The cousins play card games to pass the time. At last, it is time to head to Camp Nou. The subway, which stops near the stadium, is packed with people going to the game.

Antonia (left), Gabriel, and Marta are excited to go to Camp Nou. They try to wait patiently for their parents to take them to the game.

When Antonia arrives at the stadium, she is surprised by the number of fans who have also come to see the game.

Antonia and her family are big fans of *fútbol,* and they cheer during the game. When the crowd sings the team song, it is loud, especially at the end when everyone chants "Barça! Barça!! Baaarçaaa!!!" Neither team scores a goal during the first half of the game. Near the end of the second half, Antonia's favorite player, Reina, passes the ball to one of his Barça teammates, Abelardo, by hitting it with his head. Abelardo kicks the ball directly into Real Madrid's net. With that, Barça wins the game 1–0. The crowd goes wild, cheering and stamping their feet.

After the game, Mamá takes Antonia and Felipe to the Barça souvenir shop. Both of them are grinning from ear to ear when they come out wearing new red-and blue-striped shirts, just like the Barça players wear.

When they get home from the game, Antonia and Felipe's father prepares *bocadillos* with *mortadela.* Antonia gobbles her food. She knows her friends are already outside playing *fútbol,* and she can't wait to join them with her cousins and brother. After the meal, the children ask to be excused and run outside to play. With Antonia's friends, they practice the *fútbol* kicks they saw at the game earlier. Antonia scores two goals!

Soon, it is time for Gabriel, Marta, and their parents to leave. Antonia is sorry that they have to go, but she knows she will see them again in a few months.

Antonia, Felipe, and their parents spend the rest of the evening watching television and having a light dinner. When Antonia and Felipe yawn, Mamá says, "It's been a long day for both of you. Time for bed." Antonia and Felipe are tired but happy. *"Buenas noches,"* they say to their parents, "and *gracias.*" It is not long before Antonia and Felipe fall asleep wearing their new shirts, and dream of becoming famous soccer players.

Glossary

abolish To cancel or do away with

ancestor A person from whom one is descended

aqueduct A bridge-like structure with a long pipe that brings water from far away

caravan A group of travelers journeying together, often for safety reasons

civil war A war between different groups of people or areas within a country

culture The customs, beliefs, and arts of a distinct group of people

custom Something that a group of people has done for so long that it becomes an important part of their way of life

denomination An organized religious group within a faith

dialect A version of a language

discrimination The act of treating people unfairly because of race, religion, gender, or other factors

execute To put to death

flamenco A rhythmic style of music and dance

homeland An area that is identified with a particular group of people

immigrate To settle in a different country

insulation A material that prevents the passage of heat, electricity, or sound into or out of a place

invasion The act of entering with force

irrigation The process of supplying water to land

lance A long wooden spear-like pole with a sharp iron or steel head

livestock Farm animals

mosque A Muslim place of worship

occupy To invade and control a country, as by a foreign army

parliament The lawmaking body of a country

persecute To harm another person for religious, racial, or political reasons

port A place where ships load and unload cargo

prophet A person who is believed to speak on behalf of God

stigma The part of a plant where pollen is deposited

suburb A residential area outside a city

synagogue A Jewish place of worship

territory An area of land or water within a country ruled by an outside country

terrorist Using violence to intimidate societies or governments, often for political reasons

Index